Philosophy for beginners

How to understand the basics of philosophy as easy as child's play and successfully apply them in your everyday life by means of practical exercises

Jakob Schröter

CONTENT

What you can expect in this book

Philosophy - the term sounds fascinating, beautiful, somehow romantic and harmonious, and at the same time like great intellectual effort. Yet philosophy is actually neither particularly romantic nor particularly strenuous.

It's true that you have to use your brain, and perhaps some things are beyond normal common sense, but basically philosophy is just being interested in people and the world. The image one has in one's mind of ancient Greek philosophers strolling in their long robes in the Athenian sun while exchanging their thoughts may seem romantic, but they often dealt with serious topics and many did not only make friends with their sometimes revolutionary thoughts.

However, philosophy is absolutely not "old hat", but a spiritual science that has run through the development of mankind since ancient times and has significantly created the society in which we live today. Moreover, the central themes of philosophy are as relevant today as they were then and can make a valuable contribution to the world and to each individual in order to develop positively.

In this guide, I would like to give you a first insight into the great subject of philosophy and also bring it closer to you practically. After an explanation of what philosophy is exactly and what it deals with concretely, I would like to introduce you not only to some important philosophical currents and wisdoms of the philosophers, but also give you some exercises and tips on the way so that you can easily integrate philosophy into your life.

For the love of wisdom

Have you ever wondered how the world could be made more just, what is right and wrong, or what behavior is morally right or wrong? Do you sometimes think about whether there is a God or a higher plan according to which events in the world take place? Do you worry about the importance of nature, what love is, or what the meaning of life is? Or do you wonder what really matters in life, what happiness is and how to achieve it? This means that you think about the world and your own life, so you don't just accept everything without questioning it. This is very good, even if it may give you headaches more often, because it means that you are using your mind - and thus you are already a little philosopher. Perhaps you have already realized this and that is why you bought this book to expand your thinking, or you hope to find answers to your questions through the wisdom of older, well-known philosophers.

Both are possible - but this right away: Philosophy means "love of cleverness", not "cleverness" itself. So you will find in this book many thoughts with which you can answer your questions if you want, but which are primarily suggestions to think for yourself.

Because "love of wisdom" means that you go in search of wisdom, but not necessarily that you find definitive answers. However, with every thought you become a little wiser and so I invite you to dive into the world of philosophy, to take old thoughts with you and develop new ones from them.

Enjoy reading, learning and philosophizing!

Basic concepts of philosophy

What do you have to do to be a philosopher? Not much, really - just think. Basically, what you do all the time anyway. However, there is a difference to "normal" thinking, because this usually deals with everyday unnecessary things, such as what to buy, what clothes to wear to the party or why your colleague doesn't like you. Thinking philosophically, on the other hand, means questioning the world and thinking about the things in life that really matter.

Even though this may sound very intellectual, I would like to claim that pretty much everyone has philosophized at some point. Because as complicated as some philosophical thoughts may seem (or be), they usually start with a question that is an everyday part of life. The goal is reflection itself, and this is how the philosophers of past centuries and millennia have always nudged each other, questioned each other, and further developed each other.

WHAT IS PHILOSOPHY?

Philosophy deals with life and everything that constitutes and influences being human and human coexistence.

Beyond that, however, it is also about the right behavior in relation to the world, the logical connections of world events and thinking itself. Virtue, ethics, morality and logic are central aspects of any philosophy. The endeavor of philosophy is thus to better understand everything that happens in us and around us and to find the "right" way for one's own actions. Topics range from our own physical existence to happiness, justice, science, religion, and the universe. Examples of philosophical questions are:

What is love?
What is happiness?
What is justice?
What is freedom?
Why do we die?

Where do we go when we die?

Is there such a thing as destiny?

What can we know?

Is there a higher meaning to what is happening?

Is it ethical to eat meat?

Where is the end of the universe?

Are there parallel dimensions?

Do things really exist or is everything just imagination?

Who gets to rule over others?

Why do we think?

What is morally right and wrong?

How are body and mind connected?

Is there a God?

Is man allowed to interfere with nature?

What is the meaning of life?

These are only a few of countless possible questions as they occur in philosophy. The basic questions are according to Immanuel Kant:

What can I know?
What should I do?
What can I hope for?
What is man?

And accordingly, the basic themes of philosophy are metaphysics, ethics, religion and anthropology. This is a further development of the topics of the Greek antiquity, in which especially virtue, truth and nature played a central role.

Basically, anything can become a philosophical question if you question it. A simple example, as it is used in philosophy classes, is the question: "Is there still mustard in the refrigerator?" Here, one initially thinks: what is philosophical about this? Either the mustard is there or it isn't, depending on whether you bought some or have already used it up. At second glance, it's a philosophical problem, because how would you know that the mustard is in the refrigerator if the refrigerator door is closed? The answers "yes" or "no" assume that you can know what is in a place that you can't see right now. But how would you know? You only know that the mustard was there (or not) the last time you looked in the refrigerator. But who's to say that someone hasn't taken the mustard away or eaten it in the meantime? And how do you even know that what you don't see right now exists at that moment?

In human thinking, certain norms are fundamentally anchored as to how something has to be or is to be defined. These norms are trained into the human being by upbringing, the social, cultural and religious context and pass into his own thinking, so that he perceives them as self-evident and irrefutable. Philosophy goes beyond the limits of these norms, critically questions them and overturns them. If something is questioned philosophically, it dissolves into nothingness, because there is no concrete, irrefutable answer. At the end, at the latest, the question arises: But how do we know that this is really the case?

The goal of philosophy is therefore not to find a universally valid answer to the question posed in each case, but to relativize the existing norm, to trigger the thinking process and to find for oneself one's own (momentarily) correct answer. For this, the philosopher uses his intellect, i.e., he tries in a rational way and with logical thinking to expand his understanding on the subject in question.

EPOCHS AND CURRENTS OF PHI-LOSOPHY - AN OVERVIEW

As one of the first sciences, the history of philosophy goes back to the age of antiquity - that is, a few centuries before the birth of Christ. It is particularly interesting that at this time philosophical currents arose simultaneously in different cultures, each of which developed great power in its cultural sphere - and independently of each other in Greece, China, India, Persia and Israel. This is called the "axis time of world history". In Greek antiquity, philosophy and the natural sciences were closely linked, which is where the term "mother of the sciences" comes from, while in the East there was sometimes a strong connection with religion.

Already at the end of antiquity, however, the streams of philosophy ebbed away and nothing, or as good as nothing, followed in Europe for a long time, after still in the Roman Empire, which at the end also ruled Greece, among other things, the originally fought Christianity had become the state religion. Although Christianity actually conveys the message of charity, equality and tolerance, it was misused as an instrument of power in the Middle Ages.

In the Middle Ages, the Christian church dominated over the people; faith took the supreme role in society. Even the rule of the king or emperor was derived from the will of God. Anyone who claimed otherwise was considered a "heretic" and was executed. Philosophy did exist, but nothing was questioned; instead, the power of the church was confirmed.

Philosophy was thus degraded to an instrument of theology. In the Scholastic era (9th to 14th centuries), philosophical questions were asked and the pros and cons were critically weighed, but only to the extent that the limits of faith permitted. In particular, Thomas Aquinas concluded that faith and reason do not contradict each other, since they both come from God, and that God establishes the supreme law, which forms the framework for natural law and thus also for human reason. However, he also referred to the ancient philosopher Aristotle and the virtues, such as justice, fortitude and temperance, which were an important aspect of Greek philosophy.

Towards the end of the Middle Ages, the middle classes grew stronger and individuals increasingly dared to develop their own thinking.

In humanism (ca. 1400 to 1600), philosophers such as Petrarch and Erasmus of Rotterdam recalled antiquity and, in its spirit, demanded that man develop a comprehensive education, aesthetic sensibility, sincerity and political self-awareness. Henceforth, only reason and experience were to serve knowledge, so that the influence of ecclesiastical or state authority on thought dwindled.

This philosophical shift also revolutionized science - for example, Nicolaus Copernicus and Galileo Galilei researched the universe and determined that the Earth revolved around the Sun, not the Sun around the Earth, as had previously been propagated by the Church.

The next great revolution of the world view took place in the Age of Enlightenment, when, among other things, the idea of the modern state was developed from the value of freedom. We thus owe the free world in which we live today to philosophy.

In modern times, there have been and continue to be many philosophers who develop the thoughts of previous philosophical currents in relation to the world, society and human life. In this period, philosophy mainly urges modesty, offers ways to one's own happiness and calls for equality for all, especially women and men.

In the further course of the guide, I will introduce you to the most important philosophical currents and their thinkers in more depth.

Philosophy as science and personal guide

Philosophy is not only a school subject offered as an alternative to religion, but also a university course of study in the humanities. It has a difficult standing as a "science," however, because critics argue that it differs fundamentally from other sciences in the scope of its topics as well as in its methodology.

Other sciences deal with a specific spectrum of subjects, while philosophy deals with everything that falls within the fields of the other sciences and turns it upside down by questioning it. Moreover, depending on the current, it does not work with evidence and facts like the other sciences, but with thoughts alone, and accordingly creates only views and not facts.

However, it is the "mother of the sciences", because with exception of law, theology and medicine all other sciences have formed from it. Without philosophy there would be almost no sciences, because they would lack the reason of their existence. In the beginning there were the questions and with different methods, based on these questions, scientific answers were started to be searched. If one would say, philosophy is no science, one would deprive the other sciences of their basis. Because what is the point of doing research if you are not looking for answers? And if one looks for answers, it is again philosophy.

As one of the oldest sciences, it has its raison d'être in particular because it is the only one that has the power to open our eyes to virtue, morality and justice, because it does not simply accept facts and norms as such. Thus, philosophical thoughts have been a cause for fundamental changes several times in history, such as the French Revolution or the abolition of slavery, and form an important basis of our social values and structures. For example, without philosophy there would probably be no democracy, no freedom and equality of all citizens and no social system.

To call oneself a "philosopher", however, one does not have to have studied philosophy. Rather, every person can be a philosopher if he dares to go beyond the previous limits of his thinking.

However, philosophy does not exist only for the sake of "love of wisdom" (which is the literal translation of the term "philosophia") and as a means to improve the world for the community of people as well as for the natural environment, but offers each individual opportunities to make his life happier, to find his personal meaning in life and to broaden his horizons. Through philosophy, you can become more balanced and gain inner strength so that you can live a more stress-free life and better achieve your goals. By reflecting on life and the world, you can realize what really matters and become happier in the way you stop fretting over trifles and striving for things you don't have. You'll also learn to see the world as a whole and look at events from different angles, so you realize that most things aren't as bad as they feel to you.

In addition, you open your eyes to areas of the world beyond your own surroundings and think about what is important for society and the environment as a whole. In this way, you not only stimulate your grey matter, but also develop ideas about how to improve the world and the desire to make a meaningful contribution to it yourself. In this way, philosophy in turn also helps you yourself, because on the one hand you make the world you live in a little better, and on the other hand you increase your self-esteem.

At the end of the day, philosophy not only moves you to think and act intelligently, but if you start to think about it, you can pass it on to other people like the famous philosophers, so that they also use their minds and work together to create a better world. In the following chapters you will already find some suggestions and philosophical wisdom; afterwards I will give you some directly applicable exercises and tips for your everyday philosophical life.

Greek antiquity

In Greece, from the 7th/6th century BC, the first comprehensive European cultural system emerged, in which art, music, architecture, history, literature, mythology and various sciences such as mathematics, astronomy, geography, biology and physics formed a unity.

Since the ancient Greeks were seafarers and traders, they got to know other cultures, such as Babylonia and Egypt, where advanced civilizations with great knowledge already existed. The Greeks developed this knowledge further, which happened especially through the philosophers. Philosophy was highly recognized at the time and what almost everything in society and science was built on. The whole epoch of Greek-antique philosophy lasted only about 500 years and yet a very wide range of philosophical theories and knowledge was developed here, which are so well-founded that they have influenced all philosophers of following epochs and form the foundations of our society.

In this period of origin of European philosophy, being, truth, knowledge, the nature of man and his moral destiny were the central themes. The "moral destiny" means the good, the virtue, the soul and the happiness. This was summarized under "aletheia", which means unconcealedness. The natural sciences took an important place within philosophy, respectively various philosophers were natural scientists at the same time.

However, it is not so easy to generalize all this, because there were different epochs within ancient Greek philosophy as well as different views among the respective philosophers. In addition, they were specialized in different areas, i.e. one dealt, for example, more with language, one more with logic, a third more with ethics and yet another more with legal issues. Mostly they dealt with either natural sciences or humanities, but there were a few who were highly talented in both fields. These include, for example, Pythagoras and Aristotle.

PRESOCRATICS

The beginning of Greek philosophy was in the pre-Socratic period, which has its name (as can be easily seen) from the fact that it refers to the philosophy before the time of Socrates. This was considered the first great world philosopher who revolutionized thought, so that everything before him is considered merely "pre-Socratic".

The pre-Socratics were primarily concerned with the cosmos and its laws, the soul and the laws of nature. Pythagoras was not only concerned with mathematical formulas, but also developed the idea that the soul and not the body is the true essence of man. In his view, the soul is polluted by the physical and therefore man must work to make his soul pure. Empedocles held the view that the four elements of water, earth, fire and air are moved by love and hate, i.e., based on the fact that the four elements are the basis of nature and our life, love and hate have the power over how everything develops.

Democritus dealt with atoms and came to the conclusion that the soul also consists of such. Heraclitus was of the opinion that nothing can exist without its opposite, thus for example warmth not without cold, peace not without war and love not without hate.

Therefore, he considered that strife was a necessary part of life and, moreover, even the origin of the world.

Furthermore, he explained that logos is the supreme law that governs the world, and therefore wisdom consists in recognizing it. "Logos" in philosophy means as much as reason or rational thinking; from this term the word "logic" is derived. Heraclitus, however, extended the understanding of logos to mean "world principle," that is, the fundamental, higher order by which everything in the world and in the cosmos functions. Finally, however, it was the Sophists around Pythagoras who, with their relativism and skepticism, questioned everything again. They came to the view that man is the "measure of all things" and that there are two contradictory statements about every thing. Being is considered subjective and changeable, because everything beyond man is doubted.

Wisdom to take away

"Insofar as we interfere with nature, we must be strictly careful to restore its equilibrium." (Heraclitus)

"To all men it is given to know themselves and to be wise." (Heraclitus)

"It is best for man to spend life as much as possible in tranquility of mind and as little as possible in displeasure. This can be achieved by not seeking one's pleasure in the transient." (Democritus)

"The envious man harms himself like an enemy." (Democritus)

"One should remain silent or say things that are even better than silence." (Pythagoras)

"By the side of fate, the will is enthroned as the guiding power." (Pythagoras)

CLASSIC PERIOD

The most important part of ancient philosophy is the classical period between 427 and 347 BC. The major themes were virtue, ethics, reason, justice and freedom. Among the multitude of philosophers, the trio of Aristotle, Socrates and Plato are particularly noteworthy. Plato was a disciple of Socrates and Aristotle a disciple of Plato, but they held partly different views. Overall, they are considered the big three of philosophy and deserve to be considered each separately.

Socrates (469 to 399 B.C.) was a secular philosopher who was concerned with man and society. His guiding questions were: What is man? What should he do to act well? What should he do for his fellow citizens and his state community? What should he not do?

In the squares of Athens he taught his philosophy, for which he also made enemies. He did not mince words and accused politicians, for example, of having appropriated their offices by birthright or financial status. For this reason, he was sentenced to death on the pretext that he was seducing the youth and committing blasphemy. He submitted to this sentence, although his friends wanted to free him from prison, because he stood by his philosophy and wanted to defend it to the last. At the origin of his theory of knowledge stood the reading of an inscription of the oracle of Delphi: "Know thyself!" The basis of his doctrine is therefore the endeavor that people recognize from themselves what is right (and are not persuaded to it, as the Sophists did). By this alone they would then also act right. He called this approach "maeeutics," which derives from the Greek word for "midwife" (his mother's profession), because his philosophy was the midwife for people's knowledge.

The central themes of knowledge were virtue and the good, because only through this path, in his view (and that of many other philosophers), can one reach bliss.

<table>
<tr><td>

Wisdom to take away

"The smart person learns from everything and everyone, the normal person learns from his experiences, and the stupid person knows everything better."

"Always remember that everything is fleeting; then you will not be too happy in happiness or too sad in sorrow."

</td></tr>
</table>

"If you want to move the world, you should first move yourself."

"Only he is wise who knows that he is not."

"The story doesn't end with us."

"Right action follows right thinking."

Plato (427 to 347 B.C.) moved the gaze away from man to the eternal, which transcends him. In his view, there are "eternal ideas" and "eternal truths" that exist independently of man and of this world, that is, cosmic, supernatural laws.

According to Plato, these eternal ideas and truths should be present in every human being, since they are in the nature of the soul. Most people are not aware of them, but they can be discovered through introspection. From these eternal ideas and truths, he developed visions for a state, legal and social order in which justice, social coexistence and self-determination of the citizens prevail. After the execution of his teacher Socrates, the aristocrat's son Plato traveled to various countries, for example to Egypt, and after his return founded the Academy. This was a district about 1600 meters outside Athens, which was both a park and a place of teaching and worship, and to which only sons of aristocrats were admitted. It was not a university in the modern sense, as there were no set regulations, but there was a wide range of studies that included astronomy, mathematics, biology, and political theory in addition to philosophy. Aristotle also studied here.

Plato taught there his theory of ideas, according to which everything that man can experience with the senses arises from an original idea. These primordial images are spiritual and immaterial, while what can be experienced with the senses is only an image of the idea. Ideas exist for physical things such as trees or people, but also for values and principles such as justice or the good. The idea of the good is the highest idea, which stands above all others and in whose sense all thinking and acting should take place. According to Plato, in order to come to knowledge and thus to the good life, one must ascend from reality to the ideas. He equated this with the ascent from a cave.

The existence of man is like a cave under the earth in which people are trapped and bound and can only see a cave wall on which shadows of objects are cast by the fire. Since people have never seen the objects themselves, but only their shadows, they think that these images are reality.

When a person is able to break free from the shackles and looks around, he recognizes the objects that cast the shadows. Then he leaves the cave, is blinded by the light at first, so that he sees only shadows again, but then he gets used to it and sees not only the things of the environment, but also the sun. The latter was for Plato the symbol of the ideas and thus the deeper reason of being.

With this cave allegory, he described in a very vivid way the process of thinking for oneself, which involves a lot of effort and a great risk, but is worth it. According to Plato, the world of ideas is the origin of reality, but both worlds exist parallel to each other. While the real world, which can be experienced by the senses, is transient, the world of ideas is unchanging and eternal.

Wisdom to take away

"Those who are too smart to get involved in politics are punished by being governed by people dumber than they are."

"Nature is a letter from God to mankind."

"Thought is the soliloquy of the soul."

"Good people don't need laws to be shown what they can't do, while bad people will find a way to get around the laws."

"I don't know a sure path to success, but I do know a sure path to failure: trying to please everyone."

"The worst kind of injustice is feigned justice."

"To know oneself is the first of all sciences."

Aristotle (384 to 322 B.C.) again took a different direction, seeing the purpose of philosophy as exploring the world rationally and scientifically. He separated the scientific work and the philosophical ideal so that the two were no longer compatible, and for almost two millennia his scientific findings were considered unassailable. One aspect in particular still characterizes science today, and that is that the search for truth is the sole purpose of itself and must not have the goal of defending prejudices or ways of life.

His views and way of life often seem sober and unemotional, in many cases he is even said not to have cared about other people. In fact, he held the opinion that

God was not matter, but a pure thought entity and therefore should not contaminate himself with material things.

According to him, the aristocratic upper class therefore also had the advantage of devoting themselves to study and not having to get their hands dirty with physical labor. On the other hand, besides the Socratic and Platonic writings, it is above all his that have set timeless standards for virtue and morality. To understand this contrast, it is necessary to know that virtue, according to the definition of the ancient Greeks, implies an absence of passion, because passions, according to them, impair the mind and prevent the attainment of bliss.

A virtuous life means thinking and acting rationally and renouncing emotional and material distractions, which lead to wrong decisions and dissatisfaction. The way to happiness is to live in harmony with nature and one's own soul. This does not mean, however, that one cannot care for and love people, but that one should simply not let passions such as anger, greed, fear, envy or sadness hinder one's mind, inner peace and ability to judge.

Aristotle, then, was not a particularly heartless philosopher, but one who could control himself particularly well and thus apply his own teachings of virtue.

Wisdom to take away

"Friendship is one of the most necessary things in our lives. In poverty and in misfortune, friends are the only refuge."

"To cover a mistake with a lie is to replace a stain with a hole."

"Joy is the health of the soul."

"If there were peace on earth, all laws would be dispensable."

"He who prefers security to liberty is rightly a slave."

"Happiness belongs to those who are self-sufficient."

"The beginning of all wisdom is wonder."

"Nature does nothing in vain."

HELLENISTIC PHILOSOPHY

This was followed by the conquest of Greece by Alexander the Great and later by Rome. Philosophy was displaced from public teaching and state recognition into the private sphere, but it still gave rise to two major currents, Stoa and Epicureanism. The Stoa was founded by Zeno of Kition, who began teaching Stoa Poikile around 300 BC in the Athenian portico that later gave its name to the current.

Epicureanism is based on the philosopher Epicurus. Both currents arose at the same time and are opposed to each other. Although both, in terms of the whole philosophy of the era, had the goal of directing the conduct of life to wisdom, but with contrasting methods.

While the Epicureans chose the "pleasure principle," that is, to feel pleasure and avoid pain, the Stoics rejected any form of affect. Happiness could only be achieved by renouncing all passions, whether positive or negative, because ultimately every passion, even if it made one happy at the moment, was an obstacle on the way to virtue and thus to happiness, which could only be achieved through virtue. The Stoa, also called Stoicism, has become one of the most influential and powerful schools of thought in the Western world, because it provides a way to go through life calmly, to achieve one's inner happiness and not to be shaken by crises or problems.

Ethics and nature play a crucial role in this. According to Zeno, "every aspect of nature contains a force that is ultimately directed toward the good." Stoicism holds that man must act according to his own nature, which consists in virtuous behavior, and understand his own existence as part of the nature of the universe, which provides the higher, infinite structure and whose course, therefore, must not be resisted in order to find happiness.

The only bad thing in the world was unreason, which therefore had to be defeated by reason. Roman philosophers continued to advocate the teachings of Stoicism, but hardly developed them further; Lucius Annaeus Seneca is particularly worth mentioning here.

Wisdom to take away

"Not in the great lies the good, but in the good lies the great." (Zeno)

"The goal of life is to live in harmony with nature." (Zeno)

"Infinite is the time of the past and of the future; the time of the present is limited." (Zeno)

"Happy is not he who seems so to others, but he who thinks himself so." (Seneca)

"The greatest wealth is to him who is poor in desires." (Seneca)

"If you submit to nature, you will never be poor; if you submit to opinion, you will never be rich." (Seneca)

"Whoever steps up to the mirror to change has already changed." (Seneca)

"It is not because it is hard that we dare not do it, but because we dare not do it that it is hard." (Seneca)

Far Eastern Philosophy

While most of the philosophies of the East were closely interwoven with the religions there, two philosophies oriented to the life of man, Taoism and Confucianism, emerged in China in the last centuries before Christ.

The third major current of the Far East was Buddhism. Although the latter and partly also Taoism are understood as religion, this was not the original intention, and therefore we will only deal with the philosophical side here. As with the ancient Greeks, nature, a morally correct way of life and inner balance play a central role in these three philosophical worldviews, although the philosophies were developed independently of each other at the same time on different continents, and here, too, the philosophical thoughts exerted a considerable and lasting influence on society.

TAOISM

When exactly Taoism (or Daoism) originated cannot be historically proven. It is believed that its development dates back long before its first known writing in about 400 BC. Nevertheless, the author of the Tao Te-King, Lao-tzu, is considered the founder of Taoism.

About Laotse, whose name means as much as "old master", as much is conjectured as about the genesis of the Tao. In any case, it is clear from the Tao Te-King what Taoism means: It is a worldview and a way of life, which should show people the right "way". "Tao" translated means namely as much as "the way", even if no translation approaches the whole extent of the word meaning. For the way of Tao is not a way as it is commonly known, that is, a fixed route that has a beginning and an end, but the way of nature and being.

Parallels can be discovered with the Greek philosophers, especially Plato and the Stoics, because the Tao is said to represent the "primordial ground of all being", which is eternal, formless and unchanging. Accordingly, the Tao is the order of the world, from which the creation of all things and beings springs and with which one must live in harmony in order to lead a good life. The Tao Te-King therefore contains advice for various areas of life, ranging from health to politics to lifestyle. All human actions must be done in respect for the course of nature and in harmony with universal law. Only then can one experience virtue, power, goodness and order, which in turn automatically come to one through the Tao, if one lives according to it.

The most important principles are Qi, the life energy, and its two poles Yin and Yang. Yin and Yang are each equated with opposite qualities, for example Yang stands for energy, heat or the day, while Yin stands for calm, cold and the night. Neither is ever considered bad. The contrast is here, as with Heraclitus, also seen as a necessity of being, but unlike him not equated with dispute, but with complementation.

Also the Tao says that a thing becomes existent or recognizable only by its contrast, therefore Yin and Yang, which are to occur both in humans and in nature and each being, must be balanced. If there is an imbalance, the whole structure gets confused, which manifests itself in humans with physical or mental illness and in society, for example, with injustice or political conflicts.

CONFUCIANISM

Confucianism traces its origins to the fifth century B.C. master Kung Fu-tse (also Kong Fuzi or other spellings), who worked as a shepherd and accountant, among other things, before founding a school where he taught arithmetic, writing, music, archery, charioteering, and rites.

He did not differentiate among his students according to social status, but passed on these arts to everyone he considered worthy, although they were partly reserved for the nobility. However, he not only taught them these activities, but also trained them as human beings, and this was the real focus and challenge of his teaching. For only if the students perfected the five virtues - humanity, morality, righteousness, wisdom and trustworthiness - could they become truly "noble." Confucius himself strove throughout his life to become perfect in this respect and had very high standards for himself.

The teachings of Confucius are, in contrast to Taoism, worldly and pragmatic, there is no supernatural destiny, but the natural order arises from the responsibility of man for himself, others and the environment. Morally correct behavior, non-violence and the welfare of the people were among the main concerns of Confucius, whose thoughts in this respect partly resemble those of Socrates. In addition, he created a new image of man, for he recognized that man's actions influence society and nature. In order to be able to exercise this responsibility for the good, the development of virtues was the fundamental basis.

Wisdom to take away
"He who knows the goal can decide. He who decides finds peace. He who finds peace is safe. He who is sure can consider. He who deliberates can improve."
"Glory is not in never falling, but in getting back up every time we have failed."

"Stupidity is not 'knowing little,' nor 'wanting to know little,' stupidity is 'believing you know enough.'"
"If you make one mistake and don't correct it, you make another."
"It is better to light one small light than to curse the darkness."
"A person of strong character and moral principles will never try to save his own skin at the expense of his principles. He would rather sacrifice his life than his convictions."

BUDDHISM

Although Buddhism is counted among the world religions, there is one crucial difference from the other religions: While the latter specify a faith and a god (or gods) that believers must worship, Buddhism does not establish any guidelines.

Everyone is free to believe or not believe - this was the idea of Buddha, whose real name was Siddhartha Gautama, when he developed the Dharma (translated "the teaching"), i.e. Buddhist philosophy, around 500 BC. The son of a noble family, who came from Nepal, even said that one should examine his teachings, like everything else, on the basis of one's own experiences and judge whether one wanted to consider them right or wrong. Buddhism only became a religion in which

Buddha himself is worshipped as a god in large parts of Asia after Buddha's death (just as Confucius was declared a god after his death).

One of the highest principles of Buddhism is to judge by one's own wisdom and to believe only what one oneself recognizes as right, as well as to live and act in the spirit of ethics. In order to achieve this wisdom and virtue, meditation is considered the most effective way, because through it one can establish the unity of body, mind and soul and thus be guided by his own inner being on the right path.

The goal is the pursuit of happiness, both for oneself and for all other living beings. What is meant here, as with the philosophers of ancient Greece, is not material or transient emotional happiness, but, as in Stoicism and Taoism, happiness is seen as the state when one is inwardly balanced, at one with oneself, and satisfied with one's life, regardless of what goods or pleasures one has.

Wisdom to take away

"If you have a problem, try to solve it. If you can't solve it, don't make it a problem."

"There is no path to happiness. Happiness is the way."

"Don't dwell on the past, don't dream about the future. Focus on the present moment."

"Never in the world does hate cease through hate. Hate ceases through love."

"We are what we think. Everything we are arises from our thoughts. With our thoughts we shape the world."

"The way is not in heaven. The way is in the heart."

"Do not believe the scriptures, do not believe the teachers, do not believe me either. Believe only what you yourselves have carefully examined and recognized as serving yourselves and your good."

"Not outside, only within oneself one should seek peace. He who has found inner silence grasps at nothing, nor does he discard anything."

"All people are one. What distinguishes them is the name you give them."

Age of Enlightenment

European society in the 17th and 18th centuries was no longer dominated by the church, so life and thus philosophy were much freer compared to the Middle Ages, but kings and emperors ruled over peoples who had no say whatsoever, let alone guaranteed freedoms or basic rights. During this time, the desire for freedom and democracy developed in several European states.

The so-called state philosophers of the Enlightenment questioned the right of absolu tis tic rule to exist, developed thoughts about a political reorganization and, above all, enlightened citizens about the fact that they have their own minds, which they should use to order the state and society in the way that suits their ideas.

This philosophy gave rise to revolutionary aspirations among the citizens, which in 1789 brought about the end of the monarchy and the introduction of a human and civil code in France, while enlightened absolutism was established in Austria, Prussia and Russia, and a constitutional monarchy in England.

What the movements in all countries had in common was that they saw the rule of the rulers as power transferred by contract from the people, sought popular participation in power, and wanted to divide state power among different bodies so that it could not be abused. Within this era, there were mainly three different approaches: rationalism, empiricism, and a synthesis of the two.

RATIONALISM

The founder of rationalism is René Descartes, who revolutionized the thinking of his time by saying that one can and must doubt everything. Only in this way can one be a responsible citizen and human being and prevent authoritarian regimes from having unlimited power. According to Descartes, there is only one thing that cannot be doubted, and that is one's own existence, which is established by the ability to think.

One can see a reference back to the ancient Greeks, who considered the mind or logos to be the most important means and at the same time the goal.

Despite, or perhaps because of, his doubts about everything, Descartes was also a scientific researcher, for example in astronomy, meteorology, physics and mathematics. In his philosophy, he questioned everything that existed in the world, saying that nothing could be proven with certainty, so that everything was possibly just an imagination - not only God or other intangible things, but also material things such as the house you live in and the chair you are sitting on. Consequently, he also had to doubt his own existence, but he then came to the conclusion that he must exist because he thinks, and that thinking is therefore the only truth.

His statement "Cogito ergo sum" - "I think, therefore I am" is world-famous and famous. It follows that independent, rational thought is the key to life, and even though Descartes was initially scorned and ridiculed for his views in the first half of the 17th century, this one conclusion of his is the basis for the development of the wider, enlightened way of thinking.

Wisdom to take away

"Anything that is merely probable is probably false."

"For it is not enough to have a good head; the main thing is to use it properly."

"The whole of philosophy is comparable to a tree whose root is metaphysics, whose trunk is physics, and whose branches are all the other sciences."

"If you are too eager to live in the past, you usually remain very ignorant of the present."

"Those who walk very slowly but always follow the right path can get much farther than those who run and go astray."

"Doubt is the beginning of wisdom."

EMPIRICISM

For the empiricists, understanding was also important, but they defined it differently. The mind had limits, which lay in what is possible to know, that is, what is empirically researchable and provable. What goes beyond that, according to them, should not be the subject of philosophical work, because it would not be purposeful, since it is not tangible. Therefore, they held that scientific research should be at the center of philosophical work, similar to what Aristotle had done before. Among the empiricists were John Locke and David Hume, who is considered the father of the Enlightenment.

John Locke was not only a philosopher, but also a physician and at times a politician. The latter gave him an insight into the political events of his time and influenced his philosophy. In his writings, which influenced the constitutions of almost all liberal states, he held that the power of the state must be shared and that the government must provide for the welfare of the citizens in all matters, including their liberty. According to Locke, there are certain natural rights and laws that every person must respect.

These include, for example, the right to liberty, the right to life, and the right to health, as they are constitutionally guaranteed today but were not at the time of absolutism. In his opinion, the highest goal of a society is the achievement of the state of nature, which exists when all injustices have been abolished and perfect freedom and equality of all people prevail.

However, he also believed that people would not accept and implement these natural laws on their own, or not quickly enough, and for this reason he considered the state necessary to ensure that these laws are observed and that there are no conflicts. The power of the people should be guaranteed by the state being legitimized by the citizens in a social contract, which resembles a constitution in the modern sense. In order to establish such a state, there should be reforms instead of revolutions, since these are easier to implement without violence.

In France, Jean-Jacques Rousseau took an even more radical view. He referred to the social contract as proposed by Locke, but emphasized even more than the latter that this contract was entered into out of the free will of the citizens and that the political system thus stood and fell solely through the citizens. However, it was not the will of the individual but of the community that was decisive; this was above both the absolutist state and individual subjective interests. Therefore, according to him, it was the voluntary decision of the sensible citizen to submit to the state for the good of all, but without forfeiting his personal freedom. With this idea of the common good, he was decisively the one on whose thoughts the French Revolution was based and influenced later philosophers of state and law such as Kant, Marx and Hegel.

John Locke also developed a theory of knowledge, which states that the mind is formed only in the course of life with the experiences and is not given from birth. In this sense, he was entirely an empiricist, because knowledge, i.e. the formation of the mind, should, according to him, be based solely on empirical experiences. A development of the understanding beyond the experiences was possible, but only by combining what the understanding retained from the experiences; this means in other words that the empirical experience is the foundation stone of thinking.

David Hume also held this view and developed it further. The origin of all knowledge is sensory impressions, and everything that goes beyond this and cannot be clearly proven is to be rejected. In his opinion, there is no fixed personality, but man comes into the world as a blank sheet and forms the idea of himself only through the experiences he gathers.

Accordingly, a change of the ego can occur with every experience. He also held the view that man develops his thinking and acting from repeated occurrences, i.e. habits develop, through which man gets certainty about cause and effect. However, he clarified that there is only certainty about what has been perceived, i.e. what has already happened, while conclusions from it for the future are mere speculation and not provable, i.e. no truth. With these thoughts, he not only questioned the omnipotence of God and rulers, but also raised questions that were interesting for the psychology of later centuries - after all, he postulated that what has been need not continue or take place again, and thus neither authoritarian systems would have to remain in place nor bad experiences lead to worries about the future.

Wisdom to take away

"Happiness and unhappiness are two states whose extreme limits we do not know." (Locke)

"What our thought can conceive is scarcely a point, almost nothing in proportion to what it cannot conceive." (Locke)

"Every step forward that the mind takes in its path to knowledge brings some discovery that is not only new but, for the moment at least, the most valuable." (Locke)

"We would have much less strife in the world if words were taken for what they are - merely the signs of our ideas and not the things themselves." (Locke)

"Happy is he whose circumstances are adapted to his temperament; but higher still is he who is able to adapt his temperament to all the circumstances of life." (Hume)

"Nothing is freer than the thought of man." (Hume)

"The beauty of things lives in the soul of him who contemplates them." (Hume)

"Every effect is an event distinct from its cause." (Hume)

"Man's freedom lies not in being able to do what he wants, but in not having to do what he does not want." (Rousseau)

"The money one possesses is the means of freedom; that which one pursues is the means of servitude." (Rousseau)

"Character is not revealed by great deeds; it is by trifles that the nature of man is revealed." (Rousseau)

THE SYNTHESIS

The greatest German philosopher, Immanuel Kant, tried to combine rationalism and empiricism. He found that both had overestimated their respective means - the rationalists thought they could fathom more with the mind than was naturally possible for it, and the empiricists believed that with scientific evidence everything that was important for man and the world could be established.

According to Kant, man's perception and research end where space, time and causality have set their limits, and therefore certain things, such as freedom or God, cannot be scientifically proven. With the intellect, man can only grasp what can be experienced, but beyond that there is a "practical reason", which consists of logically deducing, on the basis of knowledge, how that which cannot be explored could be. However, this could not be presented as truth, as the rationalists and ancient Greeks did.

In his most important work, "Critique of Pure Reason," he posed the four authoritative questions of philosophy: What can I know? What should I do? What may I hope? What is man? With these questions and the answers to them, he further developed the philosophical theories of his predecessors. Metaphysics, morality, religion and science of man, i.e. the topics as already explored by the ancient Greeks, were the leitmotifs of his philosophy. Here he came to the fundamental realization that the mind was the decisive basis for everything.

However, he meant a rational mind that rationally analyzes what is true and untrue, right and wrong, or possible and impossible. For him, the mind was not the basis of physical and mental existence, as it was for Descartes, but it was the basis of mature participation in society and responsibility for one's own life, for fellow human beings and for the environment. He did not assume a higher order, as the philosophers of Greek antiquity did, but saw the understanding human being from within himself able and obliged to live virtuously and ethically correct and thus to shape the state and society in such a way that justice, freedom and political participation prevail for everyone.

In the spirit of Plato, he described knowledge as a risky act, which was a very realistic assessment in view of the still absolutist state power. His call to the citizens was therefore "Sapere aude" - "Have courage to use your own mind". This sentence went around the world and has a timeless message, namely that no effort and no risk should be spared to question and, if necessary, to change the existing in order to create a positive world for the general public. This has always been the goal of philosophy, whether in Europe or in Asia, but Kant wrote the best explained and most practicable synthesis of all ideas up to that time.

Wisdom to take away

"The aimless man suffers his fate, the purposeful man shapes it."

"Peace is the masterpiece of reason."

"Without respect, there is no true love."

"If some will enjoy without working, others will have to work without enjoying."

"One is rich not by what one possesses, but by what one knows with dignity to do without. And it could be that humanity becomes richer by becoming poorer, that it gains by losing."

"It may be that not everything a man thinks is true, for he may err, but in everything he says he must be true."

The road to modernity

The Age of Enlightenment triggered the development of philosophy to such an extent that various new currents followed immediately, representing different approaches and views; among their representatives, some were devoted mainly to the state and social order, others primarily to man and his inner being.

IDEALISM

Especially in Germany, Kant's maxims developed into idealism, whose philosophers, such as Johann Gottlieb Fichte, Friedrich W. J. Schelling, and G. W. Friedrich Hegel, among others, believed that reality is created by thinking. The world in which one lived changed depending on how one thought about it, with ideals forming the basis for knowledge and morality.

Hegel in particular went down in history with his theory. He concluded that within a human being and a state, the mind develops in such a way that an absolute conception emerges of what is real and reasonable. However, the world is in an incessant change, a process of change, in which the developments logically build on each other.

Every historical event is thus the necessary, natural consequence of the preceding situation. Thus, the world is formed in a "dialectical process of change", through which the development as a whole is always progressing. Accordingly, something bad can become something good and something good can become something even better. Hegel related this theory, among other things, to the example of God, who, or rather whose conception, in his view, did not exist from the outset in the form that it did at the time, but rather developed in the course of time through the thinking of people. According to his theory, common realities such as faith, the state or the social order are formed from the thinking of all people involved, while each person also creates the reality of his existence for himself through his thinking.

Hegel's view strongly polarized the world of philosophy - while Karl Marx and Friedrich Engels developed their thoughts on the class struggle and a socialist social order from his ideas, two currents in particular formed with materialism and positivism on the one hand and the philosophy of life and existence on the other, which opposed Hegel's philosophy but also contradicted each other.

Wisdom to take away

"The sense world we recognize, in the supersensible world we live." (Fichte)

"Man can do what he ought; and if he says, I cannot, he will not." (Fichte)

"The lie is always a suicide of the spirit." (Fichte)

"The external world lies open before us in order to find in it the history of our spirit." (Schelling)

"True greatness consists in condescension, in the ability to descend to the lowest points without forgiving one's highness." (Schelling)

"The truth of an intention is the deed." (Hegel)

> "Whoever wants something great must know how to limit himself; whoever, on the other hand, wants everything, in fact wants nothing and achieves nothing." (Hegel)
>
> "To action belongs essentially character, and a man of character is a decent man who, as such, has definite aims in view and pursues them with firmness." (Hegel)

MARXISM

Karl Marx brought philosophy to a new reality, because he believed that the meaning was not merely to think about the world, but to change it. The main content of his philosophical work was the social situation of the people of his time. He saw that most people worked hard without getting enough money for it, while a few others lived in great prosperity without doing anything for it.

His goal was to open people's eyes to social injustice, and he developed a vision of a society without class distinctions and without exploitation. He predicted that the unjust situation that existed at the time would lead to the revolution of the proletariat (the working class) and a communist state would be established. Together with his friend Friedrich Engels, who was actually a factory owner's son but sided with the workers, he elaborated the idea of communism into a political concept.

In this form of state, everyone should own the same amount, everyone should have the same rights, and all property should be common property. Her "Communist Manifesto," published in 1848, became the starting point for several revolutions after her death and led to the establishment of a communist state in Russia in 1917.

Wisdom to take away

"But man, that is not an abstract being squatting outside the world. Man, that is the world of man, state, societ." (Marx)

"The demand to give up the illusion about one's condition is the demand to give up a condition that needs illusion." (Marx)

"It is not consciousness that determines life, but life that determines consciousness." (Marx)

"No man fights freedom; at most he fights the freedom of others." (Marx)

"Everything that sets men in motion must pass through their heads; but what form it takes in that head depends very much on circumstances." (Engels)

"Where there is no commonality of interests, there can be no commonality of goals, let alone of action." (Engels)

"If man is formed by circumstances, then circumstances must be formed humanly." (Engels)

MATERIALISM AND POSITIVISM

This current, launched in the mid-19th century by Auguste Comte and Ludwig Feuerbach, rejected Hegel's approach as too speculative. Their opinion was similar to empiricism, for they, too, were of the opinion that metaphysics should play no role in philosophy, but that all thinking must refer to the materially existing, since only its truth could be positively ascertained.

However, the term "material" is not only referred to physical things, but in their opinion everything consists of matter, thus also thoughts, feelings and the consciousness, because their currents are physically measurable. Everything which is not measurable and therefore has no matter, could not exist accordingly. For this reason the materialists negated the existence of God. For Feuerbach, God was replaced by politics, which gave man the possibility to create in reality the life he had previously dreamed of by believing in God.

Wisdom to take away

"Science leads to foresight; foresight leads to action." (Comte)

"Live a life open to all." (Comte)

"To a perfect man belongs the power of thought, the power of will, the power of heart." (Feuerbach)

"We are with books as we are with people. We make many acquaintances, but we choose only a few as our friends." (Feuerbach)

PHILOSOPHY OF LIFE AND EXISTENCE

At about the same time, the philosophy of life developed around Friedrich Nietzsche and Henri Bergson, among others, as well as the existential philosophy around its founder Søren Kierkegaard.

The main statement of the philosophy of life was that philosophy previously could not really relate to life because it had been too stuck in generalizations, narrow conceptualizations and abstract systems of thought. These could not, for a long time, take into account the breadth of human existence and, in particular, emotions, and in this respect could not be a true aid to further development and understanding of human and social processes. Therefore, in her opinion, philosophy should be exercised through intuition and poetic language.

The existential philosophers were concerned with human existence and tried to fathom how it develops and what its meaning is. Kierkegaard, who was not only a philosopher but also a theologian and psychologist, introduced an aspect into philosophy that had never been considered before, namely fear.

This realization was probably the conclusion of his psychological and theological background as well as his own melancholy inherited from his father. He thereby distinguished anxiety from fear, since fear, in his view, was related to a specific thing, while anxiety occurred without external cause, and made it clear that anxiety was something completely natural that occurred in every human being. Fear itself, he said, is neither negative nor positive, but it can lead both to "sin," as he called it, referring to a biblical context, and to positive possibilities. For fear confronts man with a decision and is thus the epitome of freedom. According to Kierkegaard, there can be no freedom without fear. When one is afraid, one is finally faced with the choice of how best to behave: Either one gives in to the fear and withdraws inactively, or one allows oneself to be seduced into taking risks, or one rationally considers how one can best take advantage of the situation.

Thus, fear can be seen as a motor of human development - how this development looks like is then up to each person himself. Also the subjectivity of thinking, feeling and deciding is a central statement of Kierkegaard. Every person sees himself and the world differently and also acts differently on this basis. Accordingly, changing subjective perception is a prerequisite for using fear as an opportunity. With these observations, Kierkegaard provided an authoritative basis for psychoanalysis and behavior therapy.

Among the existential philosophers was also Martin Heidegger, who dealt with the question of the existence of being in his work "Being and Time" in 1927. He saw the confirmation for this in the fact that the human being exists spatially, both at the actual place and in the world, and from this spatial existence a temporal existence results. Today's philosopher Peter Trawny explains that what is meant by this is that human existence includes an openness to the world and, conversely, that man needs the openness of the world for his existence.

The writers Jean-Paul Sartre and Albert Camus are also among the philosophers of existence. Sartre (1905 to 1980) held the view that man is the only being aware of his existence and for this reason is condemned to freedom, so that he himself is responsible for his thoughts and actions.

However, he also saw a great opportunity in this curse, namely to live as one wants and to create the world according to one's own ideas. According to this, you don't have to simply accept anything and can change both your own behavior and society. Albert Camus developed the "Philosophy of the Absurd" in 1942. He did not want to be counted to existentialism, but he will be because of his view that the world is fundamentally absurd and senseless, so that it could never be understandable for man. He said that man could accept the feeling of absurdity and be spiritually above it, so that he would retain his dignity; later, however, he suggested that people should rebel against the absurd in order to preserve their dignity. In all this, he was particularly concerned with the question of how man can act properly when he is on his own, that is, when he receives no help from God.

Wisdom to take away

"Comparison is the end of happiness and the beginning of discontent." (Kierkegaard)

"The world, flawed as it is, is nevertheless beautiful and rich. For it consists, after all, of nothing but opportunities for love." (Kierkegaard)

"Faith consists in clinging to the uncertain with passionate conviction." (Kierkegaard)

"It takes courage to want to show yourself as you really are." (Kierkegaard)
"The most alarming thing in our alarming time is that we do not yet think." (Heidegger)
"Language is the house of being." (Heidegger)
"Laugh at life! Perhaps it laughs back." (Sartre)
"There are a lot of people in the world who are in hell because they depend too much on the judgment of others." (Sartre)
"Man is nothing but what he makes of himself." (Sartre)

WOMEN IN PHILOSOPHY

In recent decades, the development of philosophy has not stood still, but neither (from a current perspective) has it produced any groundbreaking findings - with one exception: recently, the female gender has no longer been denied the ability to philosophize.

As much as the philosophers of the past millennia were busy exploring sense and nonsense, being and non-being, justice and injustice, wisdom and ignorance, the vast majority of them could not get out of the entrenched thinking of their time with regard to gender roles. Women were not capable of being philosophers, postulated even those who were not explicitly misogynistic. Few exceptions were, for example, Pythagoras, who taught both men and women in his teachings, and John Stuart Mill, who was the first European parliamentarian to demand that men and women should have equal rights.

This does not mean that there were no women philosophers, but that they were not heard and probably most of them remain unknown to this day. The general development of recent history, in which equality is constitutionally guaranteed and feminist movements have brought about a revolution of thought (of many, but far from all), has as a logical consequence that women are also accepted in philosophy.

But just as there is no equality of income or balanced distribution of both sexes in all occupational groups for a long time, the development process in philosophy has been initiated, but is still far from reaching its goal. In order to do justice to women in philosophy as well, I would like to conclude by introducing you to a few of the few well-known female philosophers:

Hypatia of Alexandria was the only famous philosopher, mathematician and astronomer of ancient Greece. She was celebrated as a witty thinker and scientist and was the only woman to teach her doctrines publicly. Among other things, she established even then that the earth orbits the sun. However, her knowledge was forgotten for almost two millennia after she was cruelly murdered.

Émilie du Châtelet was a mathematician and philosopher during the early Enlightenment. She held the view that everyone could do something for their happiness, no matter what social class they came from. She saw the pursuit of education as a central aspect of happiness. She also criticized the role of women at the time and emphasized that women should have the same rights as men.

Hannah Arendt studied philosophy with Martin Heidegger, among others. When the National Socialists came to power in Germany in 1933, the young Jewish philosopher fled to the USA. In her writings, she addressed in particular the human rights of political refugees, political violence and its origins, the incomprehensibility of evil, and the meaning of work.

Simone de Beauvoir was the companion of Jean-Paul Sartre, whom she had met during her studies. Originally individualistic, after he had been a prisoner of war in Germany, she developed existentialist thoughts and also the ambition to use her philosophy for solidarity, social and political purposes. In contrast to Sartre, she also thought about morality in existentialism. However, she did not see herself primarily as a philosopher, but as a writer.

Wisdom to take away

"A feeling is a commitment that transcends the moment." (de Beauvoir)

"One is not born a woman, one is made one." (de Beauvoir)

"A world that is to have room for the public cannot be built for only one generation or planned only for the living; it must transcend the life span of mortal men." (Arendt)

"The sad truth is that most evil is done by people who have not decided between evil and good." (Arendt)

"To be happy, one must have laid aside one's prejudices and retained one's illusions." (du Châtelet)

"Let us choose for ourselves our path in life and let us try to strew it with flowers." (du Châtelet)

"Understanding the things that are right outside our door is the best preparation for understanding the things that are behind it." (Hypatia)

"Defend your right to think. To think and be wrong is better than not to think." (Hypatia)

Philosophical exercises and tips for everyday life

Here now the tips and exercises promised at the beginning, with which you can integrate philosophical thinking and action into your everyday life. These are just a few ideas, which at the same time can inspire you to develop your own ideas for philosophical exercises - in the spirit of philosophy, in which nothing is conclusive.

WRITE DOWN THOUGHTS

If the ancient and more recent philosophers had not recorded in writings what they developed in their minds, no one would know anything about their philosophy today. Some, such as Kierkegaard, even kept diaries.

This makes sense, because all thinking takes place in the head, but it goes so fast and is often overlaid by other thoughts that much is lost or disordered if you try to capture it only in your head. Writing down your thoughts can help to organize them, bring structure to them, and help you to see connections so that you can develop them better. In addition, you then not only recognize your own inner processes, so that you understand yourself better, but you also already have a written collection, in case you someday get the idea to share your thoughts with the world.

Since thinking usually does not come or go on command, but rather thoughts often suddenly and unexpectedly flash through your mind, I recommend that you always carry a small notebook and pen with you. Although handwritten writing has become "out" nowadays, it is more in line with the traditional spirit of philosophy and the notes are preserved even if technology fails.

You don't have to keep a consistent diary, because you may not think of anything worth writing down philosophically for a few days, and it's usually because the joy of doing something is spoiled by the compulsion. So just carry your notebook with you and write whenever the thoughts come to you.

DISCUSS

Another method, which goes back to the origins of philosophy, is discussing. If philosophers of the same and different opinion had not talked with each other about their thoughts, then everyone would have developed his own theories only for himself (which was admittedly also partly the case).

Through the exchange with others, it is possible to develop one's own thoughts further by including aspects that one has not thought of oneself. Also, one can look at one's own theories from a different perspective as one listens to others' opinions about them. While it is said: "Many cooks spoil the broth," but this is true only in those areas of life where different ideas cannot be applied at the same time, such as in cooking, crafts, or education. In science, however, and especially in philosophy, different ideas and approaches are an enrichment, as one can advance each other and develop a variety of results.

And last but not least, it's fun to discuss questions that concern you with friends. So find one or more people in your environment who are also interested in philosophy and sit down regularly in small discussion groups to exchange your thoughts.

LIVE WITH MIND

"Have the courage to use your own mind" - this applies not only to politics and society, but also to your own life. Most people simply live their lives without reflecting on themselves. This is a reason for carelessness with regard to one's own health, mental condition and the meaning of life.

One thinks, feels and acts, but in an uncontrolled way - or, better said, in a wrongly controlled way. If you don't think about your own thoughts and feelings, you do so according to certain patterns that are unconsciously imprinted by experience over the course of your life. These patterns then determine what you think and feel in which situations and what your general state of mind is. In the same way, acting takes place in schematic, unconscious sequences. You do it that way because you have always done it that way or because others do it that way.

These stored inner and outer constraints rule you, just as the citizens were ruled by the monarchs in the times of absolutism. You are not aware of the fact that your entrenched schemes partly have a detrimental effect on your life or simply do not correspond to what you actually want in your inner being, and so you do not change them, even if you have the vague feeling that you are not satisfied with something in your life. Therefore, whenever you think, feel or do something, ask yourself: Why am I thinking, feeling, doing this? Do I really want this? What do I want instead? How can I achieve this? These questions are the basis for a self-determined life.

CHANGE OR ACCEPT

An important piece of wisdom that goes back to Stoicism is: You have to accept the things that you cannot change. Otherwise, you will wear yourself out with constant negative thoughts, despair and unhappiness. Instead of wasting your energy on thoughts about unchangeable events, you should use it for more meaningful things.

This does not mean that you should accept everything that happens to you and in the world without contradiction. The motto is, "Change what you cannot accept, and accept what you cannot change." So if you are upset or saddened by a condition in your own life, in your environment, or in world events, think about whether it is within your power to change that condition. If the answer is "yes," then think constructively about what you can do to make a positive change. If the answer is "no," then make friends with the situation, because if something cannot be changed, according to the ancient teachings, it is part of the universal course of things, which has a higher meaning that we humans do not always understand.

Instead of falling into negative thoughts and thinking pointlessly about how you could change the unchangeable, think instead about how you can best live with this state so that it has no disadvantages for you. Always keep in mind: the biggest disadvantage is the negative thoughts themselves, because they make you feel bad and powerless. Therefore, it is important to focus your thoughts on positive aspects of the situation or positive goals that can be achieved despite the situation.

CONSIDER THE CONSEQUENCES OF YOUR BEHAVIOR

"Do unto others as you would have them do unto you," says an old proverb quoted by Kant. In order to ensure more justice and a sustainably better world, and to be at peace with yourself, this maxim should be your constant companion.

Every behavior of a person can potentially cause harm to other people or the world; one should be aware of this. Everything cannot be considered and some is unavoidable, but one can adjust one's actions so that they can cause as little harm as possible. For example, we harm the environment in our daily routines by using water, electricity, heating, factory-made products, and driving cars, even if we don't directly notice our impact.

You can't avoid everything, but you can, for example, make sure that you don't use resources wastefully, get electricity from renewable sources, drive an economical car and as little as possible, and don't throw things away unnecessarily and buy new ones. The important thing is to think about what consequences your actions might have for other people and nature, so that you can go through life with more awareness and in this way reduce the likelihood that you will actually cause harm. There is no certainty about this, but responsible behavior in itself also counts. In particular, of course, it is important not to intentionally harm anyone or anything, for example, not to physically or verbally assault anyone, discriminate against anyone, or throw trash in the landscape.

RECOGNIZE INJUSTICE - SHOW COMMITMENT

Even though many philosophers and other people before our time have tried to make the world a just place, it is far from being so - not only in a global sense, but also on our own doorstep. One topic of your philosophical thoughts should therefore be to think about where injustice exists everywhere, starting in your immediate environment and ending in the global world, how it manifests itself and how it could be reduced.

Injustices are not only social inequalities, human rights violations or exploitation, but also, for example, bullying among colleagues or the abandonment of animals on the highway. You can stop very few of the unjust conditions yourself directly, but you can consider how you can contribute to a fairer world within the scope of your possibilities. For example, you can help with a social project in your area, buy Fairtrade products, donate money to an animal welfare organization, or make sure that no one in your circle of acquaintances and colleagues is excluded or offended.

By showing commitment to justice, you not only improve the world, but also your self-esteem as you do something meaningful for others.

THINKING ABOUT WHAT REALLY MATTERS IN LIFE

Man spends a lot of time chasing money and material things and competing for recognition among his peers. Moreover, he often gets stuck in negative thoughts about the past and worries about the future. Thus, one is hardly ever satisfied, because one is mainly preoccupied with what causes one bad feelings and what one supposedly needs to achieve. Between the dull thoughts about the past and the future, there is practically no room for the moment you are living in, and while you are rushing after external "values," you forget your inner self and the intangible gifts of life.

Therefore, you should go within yourself and realize what is really important for you, regardless of the opinion you have adopted through general social views. The ancient Greek and Chinese philosophers already knew: Happiness does not lie in the external, not in the material and not in the past or the future. Only in one's own inner being, in constant immaterial values independent of external changes and in the present moment can one find and experience happiness.

RECOGNIZE AND STOP DISHONE-STY

"It may be that not everything a man thinks is true, for he may err, but in everything he says he must be truthful," Kant recognized, and Fichte knew that lying is a "suicide of the spirit." Truth has always played a major role in philosophy, first as the goal of science and the fathoming of being, and second as the core aspect of virtue.

A virtuous life involves not only just, morally right actions, but also sincerity and bravery. You demonstrate both when you are honest - both with others and with yourself. Lying is usually done to gain an advantage or avoid a disadvantage, or you deceive yourself because you can't handle the truth.

Being honest means being brave in that you admit to yourself and others that you have done something wrong or disagree. You have to reckon with criticism, make up for your mistake if necessary and have the feeling of shrinking a little and being less "good". In reality, however, it makes you better and bigger because you show respect for others, conquer your fear of being put at a disadvantage, and face the facts, which can also mean that you have to work on yourself and make an effort to do so. For practice, do some soul-searching and think about the situations in which you tend to lie to others or to yourself, and try to avoid that in the future.

EDUCATION AND BROADENING HORIZONS

You probably remember that philosophy means "love of cleverness". The mind of a philosopher seldom stands still, and when he is not pondering existence or the meaning of the world, he is researching and educating himself, because the more you know, the more you can understand.

You don't need to develop new mathematical formulas or study quantum physics to do this; it's all about expanding your knowledge. For example, you can learn about other cultures, read non-fiction books on various topics, or simply listen to the news, think critically about it, and develop your own opinion. You can also actively experience education by traveling to other countries, visiting museums, or asking older people about historical events they have witnessed. You can also ask friends and acquaintances about their different professions and beliefs, or take trips to nature, observe the animals and plants, and think about how this natural life has developed over millions of years on our planet.

Conclusion: I think, therefore I am - or not?

Thought as the key to existence - this is probably the great commonality between (almost) all philosophers, albeit in very different interpretations. Descartes saw his thought movements as proof that he was a real being and not just a fantasy made of air.

David Hume said that thought is the greatest freedom a human being can have - in an era when human freedom was recognized as an essential aspect of existence. Buddha even said that man creates himself and the world with his thinking - a thesis that was also taken up again in idealism and existentialism.

Kant saw the application of the intellect, i.e. rational thought, as the basis for citizens to change society - and thus their existence - in their own sense. Plato understood thinking as the highest form of communication and self-discovery, it should finally be a "self-talk of the soul". Hypatia knew that free thinking is a right that must not be given up at any price.

Whether we now think as physical matter, as soul (with or without matter) or nevertheless simply as imagination of ourselves, will probably remain an eternally disputed philosophical question. In the end it doesn't matter - because "we", whatever that is, think. So some "being" of us must exist, and if it is only the thoughts themselves.

How you want to define "thinking" and which questions and topics you think about is entirely up to you. The philosophers of past times also simply thought what and how they wanted to think - such is the nature of philosophy. However, like a common thread running through the epochs of history and the various cultures is the goal of better understanding being and the world, and the intention of making oneself a better person and the world a better place. In this sense - to quote Kant again: Have courage to use your intellect.